work that God sees

prayerful motherhood
in the midst of the overwhelm

----
c a p a b l e
----

shannon guerra

Copyright © 2019 Shannon Guerra

All rights reserved. No part of this book may be reproduced in any form or by any electronic or mechanical means, including information storage and retrieval systems, without permission in writing from the publisher, except by reviewers, who may quote brief passages in a review.

ISBN 978-0-9600921-1-6
ISBN (ebook) 978-0-9600921-2-3

Scripture quotations are from the ESV® Bible (The Holy Bible, English Standard Version®), copyright © 2001 by Crossway, a publishing ministry of Good News Publishers. Used by permission. All rights reserved.

Portions of scripture in **bold** are the author's emphasis.

Cover design by Copperlight Wood

This title may be purchased in bulk for ministry or group study use. For more information, please email shop@copperlightwood.com.

Printed and bound in the United States of America

Published by Copperlight Wood
P.O. Box 870697
Wasilla, AK   99687

www.copperlightwood.com

for Renee,

who has what it takes

Also by Shannon Guerra

Upside Down:
Understanding and Supporting Attachment in Adoptive and Foster Families

Oh My Soul:
Encountering God in Honest, Unconventional (and Sometimes Messy) Prayer

Oh My Soul Companion Journal

Oh My Soul Devotional:
21-Day Complete Study
3-Day Mini Studies

the Work That God Sees series:
Prayerful Motherhood in the Midst of the Overwhelm
Capable
Allied
Growing
Steadfast
Resilient
Seen

contents

capable:
a definition
7

cover me
9

Charlotte Mason:
the Word is full of vital force
12

the overwhelm:
learning to wield it wisely
13

C.S. Lewis:
on possible and impossible things
19

like terrible people do
20

the timer
22

obiter dictum:
observations along the way
26

small spaces:
focusing on what's in front of us
27

training ground:
finding our credentials in the middle of the mess
31

George MacDonald:
on what some people think, and why it doesn't matter
35

under your feet:
overcoming the rocky path
36

Mark Twain:
for in her is that mysterious something
40

basic potato chowder
41

sweet potato chowder
gluten & dairy free
43

questions
for personal journaling or group discussion
45

notes
48

capable

capable:
adjective. able to perform

see also:
adept, adequate, competent, efficient, gifted, good enough, having what it takes, proficient, qualified

having the right stuff

this is who you are.

cover me

A glittering day. The sun is up, but not awake yet – its light is still copper, like a red-haired child with curls sticking out every which way, rubbing his eyes. Morning came early and my hair is still damp from last night's shower.

Three girls are up and bickering, requiring intervention at an average rate of two minutes per child, so in six minutes I've thrown the covers back three times. I give up and grab the coffee, and start throwing it back instead.

The day moves into breakfast, chores, lessons. You know how this goes – small details, a few more assignments every day, success gained in baby steps. Like the new blanket that will warm us in the fall, growing stitch by stitch – we work on it for a while, check our progress, but by golly, it doesn't look any more finished than it did three weeks ago. It's not nearly big enough to cover us. It's nowhere near the size it's supposed to be. And yet, there must be some progress, because I can see the colors changing.

But we are impatient. Many days it feels like we're caught somewhere between the need to enjoy the peculiarities of this season, and the need to rush some changes so we can enjoy this time more effectively. It's a weird uneasiness, this feeling of hurry-up-and-smell-the-roses.

That afternoon, on the couch with a sunburn so radioactive that NASA is probably tracking me, I'm trying to finish the last twenty pages of this Charlotte Mason book I started reading two years ago. She speaks so highly of the "power of attention and will" but I'm struggling mightily with it because five kids are right outside the open window next to me, telling stories to each other, eating lunch in a fort they made from a tarp and the patio table.

Over the clink of forks on plates and rustling of leaves in trees, I hear Iree, in an overdone British accent. "Loooong agooo, before the pushmi-pullyu was extinct-"

Andrey interrupts. "What is dat? It stinks? Eww!"

"No, *extinct*. Dead. No more of them are around anymore." I can hear someone snickering – probably Afton, that red-haired child with curls everywhere.

That night, like so many nights after the kids are in bed, we decompress and evaluate the day. Sometimes we look at the week and year ahead. We look at behavior and progress, in us and in our kids, and we wonder if the colors are changing.

We wonder if a child is ready for more freedom. We wonder if another child is ready for a new level of responsibility. We wonder about our own faith – sometimes it feels like it's not nearly big enough to cover us. It's nowhere near the size it's supposed to be.

We pray, and Vin puts it into words for me. "God, we've planted a lot of seed. We're waiting...but we're tired of looking at just dirt."

And I remember something a friend said to me recently about attachment: *The best progress is the slow progress. The best healing is the deep healing.* Growth, and grief – they both process slowly.

For the wife, sister, friend, daughter, mama – for the overrun one who finds herself crouched on the bathroom floor, elbows on knees, head in hands: When we feel like we're making bricks without straw, we run to the unruffled One who calmly used a basket of loaves and fish to feed thousands.

Never fear, whatever may happen. You are both being led. Do not try to plan. I have planned. You are the builder, not the Architect.

Go very quietly, very gently. All is for the very best for you.

– God Calling [1]

On Sunday I sat with a child who never knew how to be held by a mother, who didn't know how to relax in affection but would only submit in stiff fear: body rigid, legs unbending. She's been our very own push-me-pull-you as she learns about body space, gentleness, and appropriate touch. And now she leans, rests against my side during the church service – not in fierce pushing as before, but gently laying her head on my shoulder. She nestles there, hands folded, legs hanging off the chair, one sandal kicked off. Resting. Slow progress.

It's only because He is big enough to cover us, all of us. We can see the colors changing. Slowly, stitch by stitch, we make the blanket that warms and shelters.

> The **Word** is full of **vital force** capable of applying itself. A seed, light as thistledown, wafted into the child's soul, will take root downwards and bear fruit upwards.
>
> - Charlotte Mason [2]

the overwhelm:
learning to wield it wisely

Twenty minutes of naptime, quiet time, go-to-your-room time, I-need-to-get-adult-stuff-done time, feels like only a drop in the bucket, doesn't it? Like dollar bills in one of those wind machines, tasks swirl around in my mind and I can't grasp a single one of them.

I need to make two phone calls, but I'm already too late for one of them because Alaska's time zone is four hours behind the East Coast. I need to do paperwork for an interview. I need to think about dinner, and order new math curriculum for five of the kids, and flip the laundry. And always, always, I feel behind.

Or, let's look at another day earlier this week: I was trying to get a toddler down for a nap so I could feed a late lunch to two other kids before they needed to go down for their naps, so I could take advantage of the quiet time and finish two projects that were due in the next 48 hours.

It was a delicate chain of events with little margin for error, especially with an older kid outside who was making so much racket I wasn't sure his baby brother could fall asleep through it. He was mad about a consequence he earned, but my anger was rising, too, as time clicked on and lunchtime swiftly approached. And then fear mingled in. *If these naps don't happen, I'm not going to get this work done. I might miss this deadline, all because this kid is throwing a fit instead of helping.*

It was the overwhelm: the aggregated details of life that inundate us; the multitude of concerns and details, musts and minutiae.

The overwhelm isn't necessarily bad – it's neutral, like time or money. In strength, it teaches us focus, self-control, and discipline. It shows us what we're capable of. It teaches us to be dependent on Him. It teaches us to trust Him. It helps us develop maturity, humility, grit, and wisdom.

But in moments (or seasons) of weakness, it can leave us feeling helpless, hopeless, and fearful. Our actions are irritable and panicky as our thoughts go unfiltered: *If I had planned better, this wouldn't have happened. If I was better at this I'd be done by now. If I was more attentive to him, he might be more helpful. If I had slept less, worked harder, ignored that kid to correct the other one, been more disciplined, gotten more done ahead of time...*you know how it goes. On and on and on.

In weakness, the overwhelm puts our thoughts and responsibilities into hyperdrive, with capricious steering and no brakes.

Jesus, I whisper. Not swearing. Calling.

And it all pauses. All the thoughts whirling in the wind machine - they halt, hesitate for a moment, as though waiting for direction. That name stalls the fury.

The next day, I'm one hour from deadline, in the middle of finishing a project. Vince is downstairs with the kids and I'm upstairs with my door shut, and someone knocks.

"Yes?" I answer. A kid opens the door, and just stands there.

"What do you need?" I ask.

"I have a question," she says.

"Yes?" as my hands are still poised over the keys, and the child just stares at me. The seconds slip away.

"Yes?" I repeat. "What do you need?" But this time my tone is sharp and impatient, and the child stares at me for a few more seconds, face falling, and then says she doesn't want to ask me anymore. She leaves the room and shuts the door. And I think all sorts of failing parenting thoughts: *There goes another teachable moment. Nice job, Mama. You really had your priorities on straight that time.* The thoughts and condemnation whirl around, just like the stuff in that wind machine.

Jesus. Jesus. I keep saying His name, and the whirring slows. The thoughts wait at bay as His gravity pulls everything down to earth.

We get so easily overwhelmed. The to-do list, the bills, the kids to care for and the house to manage – we are exhausted, running on fumes, caffeine, and meals that are two hours late. We are nursing hungry babies and picking up wriggly children and hauling groceries out of the car and trucking laundry up the stairs. Our backs hurt and there's a crook in our necks from not sleeping right – or not sleeping, period – and we're not eating like we should because we're not cooking like we should, since microwaved nachos are easier to throw together than salad.

And it's not just our culture, or our busy-ness, or our family size, or the amount of activities we're involved in. No matter how simple we make our lifestyle, our days are made up of details like an afghan is made of stitches. Without stitches, you can't have a blanket; without the details that create overwhelm, you can't have a life.

He knows the overwhelm. It's why He went to the mountain, to the garden, and to sleep in the back of the boat.[3]

The Rock, his work is perfect, for all his ways are justice.

A God of faithfulness and without iniquity, just and upright is he.

- Deuteronomy 32:4

He is the Artist working intricate detail in all our days and seasons. But He wields the overwhelm wisely, as a tool to create beauty out of chaos. When we call Him, He teaches us how to make art out of our many tangled threads.

He taught Paul, too. Paul, who wrote most of the New Testament, gets it. He puts the overwhelmed mother in perspective in this passage:

Five times I received at the hands of the Jews the forty lashes less one. Three times I was beaten with rods. Once I was stoned.

Three times I was shipwrecked; a night and a day I was adrift at sea; on frequent journeys, in danger from rivers, danger from robbers, danger from my own people, danger from Gentiles, danger in the city, danger in the wilderness, danger at sea, danger from false brothers; in toil and hardship, through many a sleepless night, in hunger and thirst, often without food, in cold and exposure. And, apart from other things, there is the daily pressure on me of my anxiety for all the churches.

Who is weak, and I am not weak? Who is made to fall, and I am not indignant?

If I must boast, I will boast of the things that show my weakness.

- 2 Corinthians 11:24-30

His situation and mission were different from ours, but for our purposes, we can see that the guy was familiar with overwhelm. We have the dangers of commuting, carpooling, crowded traffic, human trafficking, internet safety, identity theft; the hassles of paperwork, Facebook trolls, broken appliances, faithless politicians, overflowing inboxes...and if we could just find our car keys on a consistent basis, we'd be winning. We pay bills, pay taxes, pay our dues, and pay the piper.

But this man, Paul, is the same man who wrote Romans 8:28: *And we know that for those who love God all things work together for good, for those who are called according to his purpose.* And while we're at it, he also wrote Romans 8:1: *There is therefore now no condemnation for those who are in Christ Jesus.*

So we can trust that God is working these details of overwhelm together for our good, and we shouldn't beat ourselves up over everything. We can put that energy into abiding instead.

It's such persons as these the world wants, persons who have worked over every acre of that vast estate of theirs which we have called Mansoul; men and women ordered in nerve and trained in muscle, self-controlled and capable; with well-stored imagination, well-practiced reason; loving, just, and true.

- Charlotte Mason [4]

I have all these kids, and I've wasted many days fighting the overwhelm as an enemy instead of as an asset. But God has given us opportunity in the mess, in the pressure, in the wind machine.

He knew how to stop the wind. He wants to teach us how to do it, too.

> When a thing has to be attempted,
> one must never think about
> possibility or impossibility....
> in war, in mountain climbing, in learning to
> skate, or swim, or ride a bicycle, even in
> fastening a stiff collar with cold fingers,
> people quite often do what seemed
> impossible before they did it.
> It is wonderful what you can do
> when you have to.
> - C.S. Lewis [5]

*Surely he was also referring to laundry day for families of nine, and shopping trips to Walmart.

like terrible people do

The first thing I did this morning was get dressed, look in the mirror, and realize I put my shirt on backwards. I am 40 years old, but somehow, something like this happens on a bi-monthly basis - an article goes on inside out, or backwards, and often it's not until the end of the day that I even notice.

Momming is so hard. Some days it catches up to us, and we look like we were dressed by our four-year-old.

I drove around town today and twice forgot to use my blinker, like terrible people do. But I am not a terrible person; I almost always use blinkers. I might confuse them with the windshield wiper sometimes, but that's also probably because I'm too tired to care if my socks match.

Or shoes. Whatever.

This afternoon I stopped to admire our toddler's shadow on the wall: the curves of his cheek, the fluffy hair, his eyelashes. His silhouette was so striking that I took a picture of it. And two hours later, I was still hanging on to how adorable he was in that photo because I was also still on the second hour of trying to get him to take a nap and he clearly would rather have been dancing the funky chicken.

And now it's the end of the day here, and I tend to over-evaluate and undersell myself every night: I didn't get enough done, I didn't make enough eye contact with each kid, I forgot to make an important phone call and completely dropped two emails and didn't write anything more profound than a to-do list.

Our little guy is up at all hours teething with molars, and I've been so tired for so long that I've forgotten to take thoughts captive and think His thoughts, which are always forward, never backward; always kind, never harsh; always productive and encouraging, never defeatist and discouraging. But He reminded me tonight. So I'm passing it along and reminding you too, in case you need it like I did.

So at the end of the evening, I am just here hiding downstairs while my kids pretend to get ready for bed (*HAHAHAHA*), taking a breather between bouts of yelling upstairs for them to quiet down.

And my only question at this point of the day is:

On a scale of 1 to Unforgivable, how bad is it that I'm letting that toddler occupy himself by using a brand new guitar string as a cat toy? Asking for a friend.

the timer

We start the day all dignified-like. A dishtowel in the kitchen hangs over the handle to the stove, and another towel hangs in the bathroom on the hook. Breakfast is eaten, chores are done, dishes are washed.

For now. For at least twelve seconds.

Daddy leaves for work and the school day commences. Three kids are at the table, three kids are all over the place, and my brain starts to scatter. Someone needs help with math, someone needs supervised, someone needs wiped, and someone needs to know if "road rash" is a compound word, totally separate words, or if it's hyphenated. The laundry needs flipped and the dishwasher needs to be emptied soon and, now that I think about it, I'm not sure if I remembered to turn on the dryer last night.

The real bummer is that I just finished my coffee and this is as alert as I'm going to get until tea time.

There are emails to answer and things that must be researched and decisions that have to be made. Follow-up phone calls and a deadline or two looming. Dust and laundry don't stop for anyone, and children who just ate an hour ago are still going to ask about the next meal in less than ten minutes. (You feel this, too?)

Aside from the daily agenda, there are so many other things we *want* to do: We want to grow veggies, harvest herbs, and learn about wild plants growing under our nose on our property. We have forts to build and needlework stitches to practice and several sewing projects in the wings. There are stories to be written and journals to be filled and a million books on our shelves beckoning for a snuggle in a sunbeam on the couch with us.

So, there is also this longing...and you know all about it. I know that you know, because we moms talk about it often.

And He knows, too, because we talk about it often, also. And He's right there, reminding me to breathe. Wait, and listen...and He says, *One thing at a time. Slow and easy. Take it in small, simple chunks. Little steps.*

I corral the little wanderers back downstairs where I can see them. We get math and dishes going simultaneously, and I start stacking plates and bowls and saucers on the counter. They can wait right there. The laundry can wait. Grammar and spelling can wait. This is life just-one-or-two-things-at-a-time, and I am running, and I can't do it all at once any more than I can put all of these dishes away in one armload.

It's still morning and we are in the thick of it: In the midst of teaching arithmetic, putting away silverware, stepping in a puddle of water, cleaning up a spill with our third dishtowel of the day, stacking pots and pans in the cabinet, throwing my wet socks in the washer, finding someone else's dirty socks on the floor, putting those in the washer too, putting away the last of the dishes, putting new dirty dishes back in the dishwasher, planning lunch, and - ohmygoodness! I just remembered – there's a child on the potty.

I'm embarrassed to tell you how long she was sitting there. But she was definitely done by the time I checked on her.

Slowly the list gets checked off. Lots of things wait until after naptime, after bedtime, until tomorrow. Sometimes they wait until next week. But what has to get done is done, and it doesn't have to be in my time frame.

And it doesn't have to be done in other people's time frames, either. We finally turned in work samples this week that were due three weeks ago...and then received a gracious note from our contact teacher (she is the sweetest ever) gently reminding us that we could turn in the progress reports any time, as well.

Oh, my word. Completely forgot about those. Coming right up...

I emailed them twenty minutes later. High five.

And then it's afternoon, after assignments, and everyone is playing. Most of the kids are outside, but the oldest and I are inside, watching his cat Gus attack his nemesis – the dangerous, the loathsome, the terrible...the tiny...Lego brick.

It is a lesson on the inefficiency of frantic motion:

Gus crouches and springs at the Lego, which flies across the room as he skids after it on the hard floor. He stops abruptly to lick his paw, idly looks around, and yowls. Suddenly he winds up for a pounce, but hesitates when we start laughing at him, and stops to look at us with an expression of wounded dignity. It doesn't last long though, because his next move is to leap on the Lego and try to eat it – but the dastardly foe is cunning and somehow escapes his grasp. Our hero races across the room and bats it around the corner, but as he attempts to follow it, his back legs can't keep up with his front legs and he spins out, careening wildly, while the Lego slides under the piano, never to be seen again.

So much effort, so little accomplished.

And sometimes, this is how my days go: Driven to distraction, reeling, careening, and then hesitating when I hear the reaction of others. With the front of me willing to start a project, but the back part of me too weak or slow to follow through.

I have to stop long enough to focus, think for a minute, and then take just the next step. We don't arrive at the mountain top in one leap.

> *And then he bent his own neck and put the chain upon it, and at once his head was bowed to the ground with the weight of the Ring, as if a great stone had been strung on him. But slowly, as if the weight became less, or new strength grew in him, he raised his head, and then with a great effort got to his feet and found that he could walk and bear his burden.*
>
> - *J.R.R. Tolkien*[6]

The Lord reminds me to focus, and go slow. It takes small steps to conquer the mountain.

The next day, we make it to lunchtime before chaos starts erupting and He has to remind me again. One child is already excused, one child is in the bathroom, and four children are at the table. I'm cleaning a puddle of accident in the bathroom to the tune of four children simultaneously requesting seconds, a drink of water, and asking to be excused.

Through gritted teeth I yell a friendly PSA from the bathroom:

"WAIT. YOU CAN ALL WAIT FOR AT LEAST THREE MINUTES. DO NOT SPEAK TO ME UNTIL THE TIMER BEEPS."

I confess I didn't actually set a timer.

I am the timer, and I refused to beep for several minutes.

obiter dictum:
observations along the way

•••••••••••••••••••••

Tired of being ignored when you want to get your kids' attention? Just yell, "Oh, GROSS!" and they will come running. Works consistently for five out of six kids in our house.

•••••••••••••••••••••

Convincing the kids that the new steam cleaner is a fascinating power tool is one of the smarter things I've done in my lifetime.

•••••••••••••••••••••

I've noticed that reading Dr. Seuss books with a toddler who doesn't turn the pages in order has no effect on the storyline.

•••••••••••••••••••••

Dear foodie blogs: It is *not* an "easy, 3-step recipe" when step one tells you to turn on the skillet, step two has nine complex sentences, and step three tells you to combine, bake and serve.

•••••••••••••••••••••

Call me an opportunist, but when a cat happens to throw up at the same time one of the kids is misbehaving, I think that's divine provision for an awesome consequence.

small spaces

focusing on what's in front of us

It was supposed to get up to eighty degrees that day in the Mat-Su Valley. Most of the kids were outside, and the three amigos – Iree, Afton, and Cham – were making a non-HOA-approved tent city in our woods out of unused flat sheets, which, in their opinion, are good for nothing else.

And I was on the couch inside, nursing a baby. Finishing a late breakfast, supervising late chores, watching the cats stalk chickadees through the window.

I rearranged the coffee table items within reach of my left arm: stacked the school books, drank three ounces of water left in the glass, and hid the pens under the couch cushion so I'd have one handy later whenever I might need it. Don't tell the kids where to find them – this is our little secret.

I spend a lot of time here and it feels pretty limiting when there's so much to do. When you can't fetch what you need, stop the cat from tearing up a houseplant, or break up a fight between kids in the garage, being confined to your spot on the couch forces you to focus on what is right in front of you.

But it's nothing compared to what happened earlier this summer. The flu rolled through all of us over a period of ten days, sparing only the baby (yay for breastfeeding) and leaving piles of dishes and laundry in its wake. It was a terrible, helpless feeling knowing there were a million things to do, but all I could do is contribute to the mess.

I mean, friends, it was scary-bad: At its peak, Vince and I and the oldest kids were all sick at the same time and completely laid flat, and our ten- and six-year-olds took care of everything and everyone for about 12 hours. They fetched and carried and got their own meals and played with the baby. They did the dishes and fed the cats and made tea and did everyone's chores. They were strong after being sick the week before, and they saved the day.

When I felt human again, I woke up at 11am to the noise of the garage door slamming and Alan Jackson playing downstairs, singing, "*And they built their house from a toolshed Granddaddy rolled out on two logs...they built walls all around it and they made that house a home...*" Vince was back on his feet and had taken the kids out for a grocery run so I could sleep, and they came home with all we needed: tons of fruit, and coffee. I nursed that coffee all day long, still sipping it cold, well into the afternoon.

> *Rejoice always, pray without ceasing, give thanks in all circumstances; for this is the will of God in Christ Jesus for you.*
>
> *- 1 Thessalonians 5:16-18*

And I'm learning (slowly) that instead of feeling defeated by everything that can't be taken care of in this moment – the 100 ounces of water we're supposed to drink, the eight hugs a day we're supposed to give the hurting kids, the four writing assignments that need checked, and the seven chapters of the book that still aren't finished – to just do what's right there in front of me.

Love the one in front of me. Drink the water in front of me. Read (or write, or edit) the pages in front of me. Whatever is within reach, whatever is right in front of you – if you can't move anywhere else, then that is your mission. Right there.

And it's not just true for the moments when we feel confined, but for the seasons when we feel hemmed in, too. We can whine about the limits or we can be grateful for the time to focus on just one thing, just one season, just the one small space we're in. Because how we handle those small spaces determines how wide they expand later.

One who is faithful in a very little is also faithful in much, and one who is dishonest in a very little is also dishonest in much.

- Luke 16:10

Seems so simple, but this is a hard lesson for me. I'm both a doer and a slacker; I confuse my slacking with resting and my doing with rushing. Who of us are objective enough to give ourselves the credit or criticism we deserve?

The only way to know is to ask Him. No matter how big or small our space is, He is always right in front of us. So we pray in these small spaces, and it is like soaking hardened water stains in vinegar instead of spending hours in pointless scrubbing. The work is practically done for us while we wait.

Continue steadfastly in prayer, being watchful in it with thanksgiving.

- Colossians 4:2

Another time, I'm stuck on the couch under a nursing, sleeping baby, and one child who has been out of control is out of my sight and I'm not sure he's where he's supposed to be. I can't check on him, but I can pray the conviction of the Holy Spirit into him, and then find out later if it worked. Same with the kids who are helping themselves to the garden hose outside without permission – pray now, assign consequences later.

We sit in our small spaces and our small seasons, and we face the choice to work smarter or work harder in them. We can pray and wait, or we can fret and spin our wheels. It is the difference between running in tennis shoes and running in oversized flip flops – we can do both, but one of them is going to make us look like a real doofus. So we'll just do what we can, with what we have, right in front of us. Sometimes all we have right in front of us is prayer, and it will be enough.

training ground
finding our credentials
in the middle of the mess

There are a lot of things I'm not good at. Don't ask me to butcher a chicken, cook a steak, or roast a pork loin (does one even *roast* pork loin? Or is it pork *loins*? I have no idea). You probably shouldn't have me do computer maintenance, or change printer ink. And if you want a buddy to go kayaking, I can point you to a dozen people right off the top of my head who would love to go, but I'll be strictly on the terra firma taking pictures of the rest of you crazies in the water.

One thing I *can* do, though, is make potato chowder. It's easy, I've made it a million times, there's nothing to it. A pot of it is cooling on the stove right now. As long as you have potatoes, cream, flour, and a tolerance for gluten and lactose, you can make any variation with broccoli, cheese, reindeer sausage, leeks, bacon, whatever.

It's not always perfect. I've messed it up before (for guests, even) and had no idea what went wrong. Probably, I was in a rush and got distracted, and got lazy on the roux. But when that happened I knew I wasn't a Bad Potato Chowder Maker; I'd just somehow made a mistake and would get it right next time. Because I am a Good Potato Chowder Maker.

But other roles are different. Like mothering.

I can do a bazillion things right all day long – do the dishes, delegate the chores, make the phone calls, discipline the kids, read the stories, break up the fight, and even cook great potato chowder – but in spite of all that, a rough episode with a kid can still leave me feeling like I have no idea what I'm doing. And a season of hard, difficult behavior from multiple kids? Not what I signed up for. I feel like the wrong person for the job.

It doesn't matter if I have 16 years of parenting under my belt and several other kids who are doing great. It feels like all those dreams and hopes I had for parenting a light, happy, loving home are out the window and that somehow in the rush and distraction of all the things, I blew it.

I know it's not true, really. I know it's just one day in a season full of difficult situations. I'm not perfect, but on a normal day I know I'm not a Bad Grumpy Impatient Heartless Mean Mama. I am a Good Mama Trying Her Best To Love Her Kids And Not Lose Her Junk.

But some days are not normal. Those days are hard, and they make me feel like a failure.

Some days are full of anger, arguing, disconnect, and disobedience, and I don't know what went wrong. Those days are a far cry from what I pictured for my family when I was younger, back when things were less complicated.

And it's not just me. I was face to face with a friend a couple of days ago, and we're dealing with the same attacks: Different situations, different histories, same hard feelings. Same confrontation with our own darkness, watching the dross bubble up so He can skim it off of us. *This isn't what I signed up for. It's not what*

I planned, and I feel like a failure because of it. God sure picked the wrong person for this job.

We argued about it the other day, God and I. Who am I to raise world changers? To encourage other parents? To make attempts to redeem the culture? I have a mess of my own on my hands and clearly I have not mastered any of this.

But He stopped me and said, *You can't comfort anyone if your life is always easy and perfect.*

You aren't disqualified because of the mess. The mess is what qualifies you. It is your training ground, giving you authority to speak into these situations because you've been there, done that, and gotten the grey hairs to prove it.

A person who goes on a journey in perfect weather and cushy camping gear isn't qualified to lead the person who's been through storms, worn holes into their boots, and had to build their own shelters along the way.

The only thing that could disqualify you is hardness and pride. Stay soft, humble, and close to Me. This proximity to Me keeps the dross from working its way back in you and becoming part of your character.

He reminded me of our marriage. About seven years in, we went through a dark time and we had the choice to become calloused, or grow closer to Him and each other. By His grace, in the moment of decision we made the right choice – and in circumstances that have throttled other marriages, somehow ours has thrived. It took several years, and we're not perfect, but we look back to that struggle as the training ground that changed us.

I have said these things to you, that in me you may have peace.

In the world you will have tribulation. But take heart; I have overcome the world.

- John 16:33

Your mess might look different from mine, but our credentials are hidden in those struggles. As long as we make it through humbler and wiser, we come out holding power, strength, and perspective that breathes life into those who need it. We're more like Him on the other side, and more like ourselves than we've ever been before. And that's our true identity.

> Some may think it was not
> the best place in the world
> for him to be brought up in;
> but it must have been,
> for there he was.
> - George MacDonald [7]

You are the right parent for your kids. Their siblings are the right siblings for them. And on rough days, they are even, still, the right kids for you.

Bloom where you're planted.
They will, too.

under your feet
overcoming the rocky path

Your feet are cold from stepping in water that someone spilled in the kitchen and left for you to mop up, and in the entire couchload of unfolded laundry, there only two clean socks that fit you. One of them is yours, but the other is one of your husband's super stretchy tennis socks. His is white, yours is navy blue with stripes; it doesn't matter.

The day ended with yelling and consequences, topped by two kids who were almost caught lying but you weren't fast enough to prove it and their track record doesn't put the odds in their favor.

These are the evenings we hide in the bathroom and slide down the wall just to crouch on the floor, done in. It's nights like these when we feel like terrible moms...or wives...or people. Because nice people don't have days like this. Nice people live in a la-la rainbow dreamland where children never lie and parents never yell and everyone gets to choose what color unicorn they want for Christmas.

That's right; it's been a terrible, horrible, no good, very bad bedtime, and you need some time to "get right with the Lord" – which translates to a crying jag behind locked doors, a huge bowl of ice cream, and three back-to-back reruns of Fixer Upper.

This is the kind of night to stay off Facebook, for the love of all that is holy. That goes for Pinterest and Instagram, too – the temptation to compare and wallow is too strong, and you are likely to run across a dozen posts by friends who want to tell you all about the food they ate while they were out on fancy dates, with their husbands, at restaurants. And you know you're supposed to love your neighbor and rejoice with those who rejoice and all that...so that's why you stay off Facebook.

> *See not the small trials and vexations of each hour of the day. See the one purpose and plan to which all are leading. If in climbing a mountain you keep your eyes on each stony or difficult place, as you ascend, seeing only that, how weary and profitless your climb!*
>
> *But if you think of each step as leading to the summit of achievement, from which glories and beauties will open out before you, then your climb will be so different.*
>
> *- God Calling*[8]

On some nights like these, I find myself wandering in circles all around the mountain: not going up, not necessarily going down, but spending a lot of energy without making any progress. And as I've prayed about it, the Lord revealed two things to me.

One: I often miss the view along the way by focusing too much on the frustrating short-term details instead of the long-term goals we are pursuing. On those days I feel like we're skidding backwards in spite of all the effort we put into climbing uphill. And it's not that we're really going in reverse; it's that my focus is in the wrong direction.

> *We all want progress. But progress means getting nearer to the place where you want to be. And if you have taken a wrong turning, then to go forward does not get you any nearer. If you are on the wrong road, progress means doing an about-turn and walking back to the right road; and in that case the man who turns back soonest is the most progressive man.*
>
> - C.S. Lewis [9]

Two: I'm more productive when I'm having fun. I do better work as a mom, wife, writer, and friend on the days when the burden is lighter – not because the burden is less, but because there are light-filled things throughout the day that are lifting it. This has a lot to do with the direction of my focus, too.

I don't just need to get right with the Lord – I need to get right with myself. Those terrible, horrible, no good, very bad bedtimes usually happen on days when I pay too much attention to the wrong things and not enough attention to the right things: like light-filled moments of baby snuggles, encouragement from friends, and kids laughing; small victories and long-term progress.

Easy to type, harder to live out. Without the sacrifice of praise, the *Thank You, God*,[10] I hike laterally around the mountain in circles, instead of actually going higher.

> *"I should like to be a brave adventurer, like Mr. Oxenham."*

"God grant you become a braver man than he! For, as I think, to be bold against the enemy is common to the brutes; but the prerogative of a man is to be bold against himself."

"How, sir?"

"To conquer our own fancies...and our own lusts, and our ambition, in the sacred name of duty; this is it to be truly brave, and truly strong; for he who cannot rule himself, how can he rule his crew or his fortunes?"

- Charles Kingsley [11]

I have often viewed the climb through a lens of fear and frustration, dreading each stone in the path because I have seen it as a threat to achievement or a sign of more difficulties to come.

Those stony places aren't stumbling blocks, Love, He says. *I made the mountain out of those rocks. They are what make your summit so high.*

It is just like Him to take the stones the enemy throws at us and turn them into a place of conquest. Those rocks are under your feet. You plant your flag there.

...for in her is that mysterious something that puts heart into soldiers, and turns mobs of cowards into armies of fighters that forget what fear is when they are in that presence – fighters who go into battle with joy in their eyes and songs on their lips, and sweep over the field like a storm –
- Mark Twain[12]

basic potato chowder

Comfort food. Fall and winter food, rainy day food. It's easy and feeds a crowd – just don't get lazy on the roux. Measurements are non-fussy estimates, so go with a smaller amount for less people, or with more for a bigger group...or if you have mostly teenage boys.

Main ingredients:
1 onion, chopped
5-8 large potatoes, diced
6-8 cups of milk. Sometimes I substitute part of this with chicken broth.
¼ to ½ cup each of flour AND butter. But they must be equal amounts. This is important. Ask me how I know.
Meat, already cooked, if you'd like to add it. We prefer ham, bacon, or reindeer sausage, or salmon with this chowder.

Optional veggies we like to add:
Some minced garlic
Broccoli, chopped
Celery, sliced
Peas
Leeks, thinly sliced

Directions:

1. Sauté the onion (and garlic, if using) in the butter on low for about...oh, 4-5 minutes.

2. Add the chopped potatoes and STIR STIR STIR to mix with the onions, roughly coating the potatoes with butter.

3. This is how we do the roux (just don't tell Julia Child) – and you need to be on top of this, so read the instructions first and then go for it. Ready? Go!

Sprinkle the flour over the potatoes and onions, and STIR STIR STIR again to coat them all with flour, which should be mostly absorbed by the butter. As soon as that flour is worked in, add 1 cup of milk and stir it in. If you played your cards right, it will start to thicken as the milk heats up. This is a good time to add any other veggies or meat you're using.

4. Continue adding milk (or broth) a cup at a time as it heats and thickens, and keep stirring. Scorched potatoes on the bottom of the soup pot are no fun to scrub later.

5. Season with salt, pepper, dill, shredded cheese (*oh YES you CAN season with cheese*, she said!), chives, thinly sliced green onions, the tears of your enemies, etc. Enjoy.

sweet potato chowder
gluten & dairy free

It's already past dinnertime, you haven't entered the kitchen yet, and you need to feed roughly half a dozen kids, including ones who can't have gluten and dairy... sweet potato chowder to the rescue. Easy ingredients, no rules, cooks fast. All measurements are approximate and all substitutions are valid. You've got this.

Ingredients:
1 onion, chopped
3-4 sweet potatoes, diced
6 cups (ish) of chicken broth
1 can of coconut milk
¾ cup corn
A tablespoon (or three, or four) of minced garlic
Pre-cooked reindeer sausage, kielbasa, other sausage (or bacon, which makes everyone happy), chopped

Directions:

1. Sauté the garlic and onion.

2. If you haven't diced the sweet potatoes yet (or your

hand is cramping and you're tired of doing it), find a kid who likes helping (and doesn't cause injuries by reckless stabbing) to do this for you.

3. When the onions and garlic are starting to caramelize, add all the other ingredients.

4. Season with salt, pepper, cinnamon, ginger, oregano, mint, dill, a bit of turmeric, whatever you like. Boom, done!

P.S. I would totally add heavy cream to this if we could all have dairy...swoon.

P.P.S. If you really want this to be easy, skip the sweet potatoes entirely (No chopping! Whoop!) and use pureed pumpkin, instead, and call it pumpkin chowder. Add cinnamon if you'd like.

questions

for personal journaling or group discussion

cover me:

What joys in this season of life do you not want to miss?

What changes do you wish you could hurry along so you could enjoy this season more effectively? Would those changes really matter in the long run?

Where do you see slow, deep healing occurring in your life? What other areas would you like to see progress in? What would that progress look like?

the overwhelm:

What kind of thoughts do you tend to have when you are overwhelmed and under pressure? Are there new thought patterns you'd like to create to help alleviate that pressure?

How can you apply the truth of Romans 8:28 and Romans 8:1 to your thought patterns? How might that change things?

How can overwhelm be an asset in your current situation(s)?

the timer:

What specific things do you currently long for as a mom, wife, friend, etc?

Do you feel an unhealthy or unrealistic pressure to make those things happen in a certain time frame?

What small steps are you taking now that will lead to huge accomplishments in the future?

small spaces:

What can you focus on today that is right in front of you, within reach?

Do any of your current routines or habits make you work harder instead of smarter? How can those be adjusted or shifted?

How is God showing Himself faithful in situations and circumstances you have no control over?

training ground:

What hopes and dreams did you used to have for motherhood? Have those changed at all? What do you dream of now?

What kind of experience have you gained through hard, messy situations in life?

How do you see God using the wisdom and character you gained from those experiences to breathe life into those around you?

under your feet:

What long term goals are you pursuing? (If you don't currently have any, now is a great time to pray about it and ask God what He sees for you.)

Are you having fun? What light-filled things can you focus on to lift the burden of your days?

Looking back, what stones in your path have become your places of conquest? Looking ahead, what does victory look like in the path in front of you?

1. *God Calling*, ed. A.J. Russell (Ulrichsville, Ohio: Barbour Publishing, 1998), entry titled "January 29."

2. Charlotte Mason, *Home Education* (Quarryville, Penn: Charlotte Mason Research and Supply, 1989), 349.

3. See Matthew 14:23 (the mountain), Matthew 26:36 (the garden), and Matthew 8:23-24 (the boat).

4. Charlotte Mason, *Ourselves* (Quarryville, Penn: Charlotte Mason Research and Supply, 1989), 206.

5. C.S. Lewis, *Mere Christianity* (New York: MacMillan Publishing Company, 1952), 94.

6. J.R.R. Tolkien, *The Two Towers* (New York: Houghton Mifflin Harcourt Publishing Company, 1966), 716.

7. George MacDonald, *At the Back of the North Wind* (New York: Everyman's Library Children's Classics, 2001), 156.

8. *God Calling*, ed. A.J. Russell (Ulrichsville, Ohio: Barbour Publishing, 1998), entry titled "August 23."

9. C.S. Lewis, *Mere Christianity* (New York: MacMillan Publishing Company, 1952), 36.

10. Shannon Guerra, "Right of Way: Giving God Room to Move," Copperlight Wood, October 2015, https://copperlightwood.com/2015/10/right-of-way.html.

11. Charles Kingsley, *Westward Ho!,* 2 vols. (New York: J.F. Taylor and Company, 1899), 1:24.

12. Mark Twain, *Personal Recollections of Joan of Arc* (Mineola, New York: Dover Publications Inc., 2002), 72.

Also by Shannon Guerra

"What makes this book stand out from other contemporary Christian writings on prayer is the author's crisp prose and sharp sense of humor. . . An insightful, honest, and genuinely funny author delivers a standout devotional."

- Kirkus Reviews

It's significant that paper is made from the same material He was nailed to. He still uses it to heal us, show us more of Him, and conquer what's harassing us.

Available wherever books are sold, and at **copperlightwood.com**

Adoptive and foster families often feel alone, but it doesn't have to be that way. Shannon Guerra learned this first-hand after she and her husband adopted two children in 2012, and she started writing shockingly transparent blog posts about what her family was going through at home, at the doctor's office, and in her heart as a mama.

And adoptive and foster families started writing back. Their overwhelming, unanimous theme was, "This is what I've wanted to tell people for so long. **I wish everyone who knows our family could read this.**"

Upside Down is the result. Because adoptive & foster families should never feel alone, & communities can be equipped to make sure they never feel that way again.

one more thing...

Do you want more encouragement in the season you're in? Do you want to grow deep and wide, regardless of your space and circumstances?

You are warmly invited to copperlightwood.com where we're transparent about finding peace in the hard moments, beauty in the mess, and white space in the chaos. It's a little unpolished here, so watch out for the Legos on the floor.

His peace is for you,

Shannon Guerra

subscribe:
eepurl.com/MugpP

connect:
instagram.com/copperlightwood
facebook.com/copperlightwood
goodreads.com/shannonguerra

www.ingramcontent.com/pod-product-compliance
Lightning Source LLC
Chambersburg PA
CBHW020628300426
44112CB00010B/1239